Lace Knitting
for Beginners

COMPILED BY **Amy Palmer**

INTERWEAVE.
interweave.com

The projects in this collection were originally published in other Interweave publications, including Interweave Crochet, Interweave Knits, Knitscene, *and* PieceWork *magazines. Some have been altered to update information and/or conform to space limitations.*

Interweave
A division of F+W Media, Inc.
201 East Fourth Street
Loveland, CO 80537
interweave.com

Manufactured in the United States
by Versa Press

ISBN 978-1-62033-576-5 (pbk.)

Contents

Reading Lace Charts

Lace knitting is fun because every row reveals a new effect—a dramatic new curve, hole, or slant. Lace lets you manipulate stitches in engaging ways and looks so darn pretty in the finished project. Some lace knitters prefer to work from row-by-row instructions, and some from charts. Working lace charts can be confusing to the beginner but is actually quite simple with some practice.

The Lace chart (at right) provides a good exercise. This eight-row, sixteen-stitch repeat uses yarnovers and decreases every other row. You can see that the symbols for yarnover (o) occur on even-numbered rows, which are the right-side rows. The odd-numbered rows are wrong-side rows and are worked without yarnovers.

When charts are worked in rows, you read right-side (RS) rows from right to left, and wrong-side (WS) rows from left to right. In this chart, Row 1 is a WS row. To begin the chart, you follow Row 1 from the left-hand side to the right-hand side, as follows: K2, p6, k2, p6. Easy enough?

Row 2 is a RS Row and introduces our first yarnovers and decreases. In this lace pattern, the stitch count remains constant. This means every yarnover (increase) is matched with a decrease so that the stitch count does not change. Work Row 2 as follows: K3, k2tog, k1, yo, p2, yo, k1, ssk, k3, p2.

The trickiest concept with lace charts is that the two stitches worked in a decrease are represented by only one symbol. When you work that k2tog, it results in one stitch but was worked over two stitches. Where did that second stitch box go?

In this case, the yarnover replaces that "missing" stitch. Once you get to the first yarnover in Row 2, you've worked all the six stitches that precede the central p2. And with the decrease, you're actually left with only five stitches preceding the p2. But you work a yarnover increase and ta-da, you're back to six stitches. When you work Row 3, there will still be six stitches on that side of the central p2.

The fact is that the yarnover is stealing a stitch box in the chart. The stitch made by the yarnover did not exist in Row 1. But one stitch has been eliminated by the k2tog, so that box creates a convenient place to show the yarnover symbol.

Although this all sounds pretty technical, it's really very simple. Just knit the chart as you see it! Work each stitch box as you come to it. You can think of the Row as representing the stitches *after* the Row has been worked—for example, the k2tog results in one stitch (therefore one stitch box) and the yarnover creates one stitch (and therefore also occupies one stitch box).

NO STITCH? HUH?

Things get more complicated when the stitch count does not remain constant. The Double Fern Edging chart (below right) shows what happens when yarnovers are not matched with the same number of decreases every row.

The first big question: What are those gray boxes in the middle of the chart? These shaded boxes are "no stitch" symbols. They are inserted in a chart when a stitch has been decreased and therefore leaves a hole where there was a stitch previously. You can see on Row 2 that two stitches are decreased (with k2togs) without compensating yarnover increases. This effectively removes two stitches from the row, leaving you two fewer stitches to work individually on Row 2 and, subsequently, Row 3. By placing a no-stitch box next to each decrease, the chart-maker is telling you, "This stitch will no longer exist and should not be worked on this row." As discussed above, the k2tog is worked over two stitches but

is represented by only one stitch box. Therefore the second stitch box, removed by the decrease, becomes the black hole we call the no-stitch box. *Just ignore the no-stitch box and do not work it.* Work the stitch before the no-stitch box, then the stitch after the no-stitch box, and continue on your merry way.

If you work Row 2, you'll have two stitches fewer than you did when you finished Row 1. But on Row 3, there are four yarnovers without matching decreases, leading to an increase of four stitches. You'll see the no-stitch boxes have disappeared *and* the right-hand end of the Row has popped out to the right by two stitches. Two of the increases have replaced the missing stitches from Row 2, eradicating the no-stitch holes, and two of the increases have added to the breadth of the row, which is represented by the chart actually growing at the right edge.

Over the course of this chart, the stitch count changes several times, including a dramatic bind-off on Row 10, which is then compensated for with four increases on Row 1. If you work this pattern, the shape of the knitted fabric will undulate with the increased and decreased stitches, creating

Tip

+ Just ignore the no-stitch box and do not work it.

a decorative edging. The Lace chart from the first example does not change in stitch count and therefore makes a better allover or interior pattern for a project.

These basic principles apply to all lace charts, no matter how complex. Just remember: A yarnover is an increase unless there's a compensating decrease somewhere in the same row. And a decrease is really a decrease *unless* there's a compensating yarnover somewhere in the same row. The corresponding yarnover and decrease don't have to be next to each other—or even close to each other—to work together.

Just have faith in the chart and knit it as you see it! 🖉

Lace

•	•	\\|	O				•	•			O		/	8
•	•							•	•						
•	•			\\|	O		•	•			O		/	6
•	•							•	•						
•	•		O	/	\\|	O	•	•		O	/	\\|O	4
•	•							•	•						
•	•				\\|	O	•	•	O		/		2
1 (WS) |•|•| | | | | | |•|•| | | | | |

	k on RS; p on WS		/	k2tog
•	p on RS; k on WS		\\	ssk
O	yo		☐	pattern repeat

Double Fern Edging

| | | | | | | | | | | | | | | | | | | | | | | | | | |
1 (WS)

	k on RS; p on WS		⟋	p2tog on RS; k2tog on WS
•	p on RS; k on WS		⌒	bind off 1 st
O	yo		▨	no stitch
/	k 2 tog on RS; p2tog on WS		☐	pattern repeat

Lady Tea Towel

BY COURTNEY KELLEY

The Lady Tea Towel is a surprisingly easy project and perfect hostess gift. A combination of simple eyelets and purl bumps creates a straightforward rectangle that calls woven huck lace to mind.

Finished Size

16" (40.5 cm) wide and 24" (61 cm) long.

Yarn

The Fibre Company Savannah (50% wool, 20% cotton, 15% linen, 15% viscose from soya; 160 yd [147 m]/50 g): natural, 2 skeins. Yarn distributed by Kelbourne Woolens.

Needles

Size 5 (3.75 mm). Adjust needle size if necessary to obtain the correct gauge.

Notions

Markers (m); tapestry needle.

Gauge

22 sts and 28 rows = 4" (10 cm) in St st.

Stitch Guide

Seed Stitch (multiple of 2 sts + 1)
Row 1: K1, *p1, k1; rep from * across.

Row 2: Knit the purl sts and purl the knit sts.

Rep Row 2 for patt.

Towel

CO 87 sts. Work in seed st (see Stitch Guide) until piece measures 1" (2.5 cm) from CO.

Next row: (WS) Work 5 sts in seed st, p1, place marker (pm), p25, pm, purl to last 6 sts, pm, p1, work in seed to end.

Next row: (RS) maintaining 5 sts in seed st and 1 st in St st at each end, work Row 1 of chart to 2nd m, work Sts 1–25 of chart to last m, k1, work in patt to end. Cont as established, work Rows 2–44 of chart once, Rows 1–44 twice, then Rows 1–23 once more. Work in seed st for 1" (2.5 cm). BO all sts.

Finishing

Weave in ends and block to measurements. 🍃

- -

COURTNEY KELLEY is co-owner of Kelbourne Woolens, distributor of The Fibre Company's artisan yarns. She lives in Philadelphia, Pennsylvania.

	k on RS; p on WS		/	k2tog		O	yo
•	p on RS; k on WS		\	ssk			pattern repeat

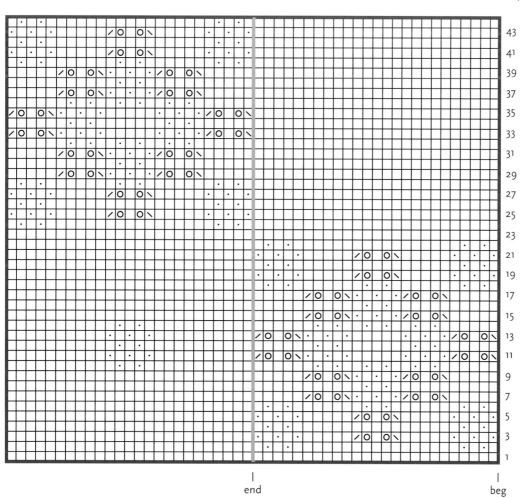

end

50 st repeat

beg

Hold Everything Tote

BY EUNNY JANG

Knitted in the round, the Hold Everything Tote combines a sturdy garter-stitch bottom and an unusual stretchy mesh rib for a bag that can hold just a couple of essentials or a whole farmer's market worth of groceries.

Finished Size

14½" (37 cm) wide and 12" (30.5) deep.

Yarn

Lion Brand Yarn Lion Cotton (100% cotton; 236 yd [215 m]/5 oz [142 g]): #136 cloves, 2 balls.

Needles

Size 9 (5.5 mm) 24" (61 cm) circular (cir) and 2 double-pointed (dpn).

Notions

Waste yarn; markers (m).

Gauge

15 sts and 18 rows = 4" (10 cm) in Lace st.

Stitch Guide

Lace Stitch (multiple of 2 sts)

Note: St patt becomes a multiple of 3 sts after Rnds 1 and 3, then returns to a multiple of 2 sts after Rnds 2 and 4.

Rnds 1 and 3: *Yo, sl 1, k1, yo, psso the k1 and yo; rep from * to end.

Rnd 2: *Drop yo, k2; rep from * to end, remove m, sl 1, replace m for new beg-of-rnd.

Rnd 4: *Drop yo, k2; rep from * to last 3 sts, drop yo, k1, sl 1 st, remove m, sl st back to left needle, replace m for new beg-of-rnd.

Rep Rnds 1–4 for patt.

Bag

BASE

With cir needle, CO 40 sts using the invisible provisional method (see Glossary). Do not join. Knit 1 WS row.

Inc row: (RS) K2, m1, knit to last 2 sts, m1, k2—2 sts inc'd. Knit 1 row. Rep last 2 rows 4 more times—50 sts. Knit 2 rows.

Dec row: (RS) K2, ssk, knit to last 4 sts, k2tog, k2—2 sts dec'd. Knit 1 row. Rep last 2 rows 4 more times—40 sts rem.

BODY

Beg working in the rnd: (RS) K40, pick up and knit 15 sts along side edge of base, remove provisional CO and place 40 sts on left needle, k40, pick up and knit 15 sts along other side edge—110 sts. Place marker (pm) and join in the rnd. Work Lace st (see Stitch Guide) until piece measures 12" (30.5 cm) from base, ending with Rnd 2 or 4. Do not break yarn. Work I-cord BO as foll: CO 3 sts onto left needle, *k2, ssk—3 sts on right needle. Do not turn, sl 3 sts back to left needle. Rep from * until all sts have been BO. Join last Row of cord to CO sts using Kitchener st (see Glossary).

Finishing

Weave in ends. With dpn, CO 3 sts. Work I-cord (see Glossary) until cord measures 36" (91.5 cm). BO all sts. Thread cord through 6 pairs of yos in last Row of lace at top of bag. Adjust cord until it is centered. Thread each end of cord through 3 pairs of yos on opposite side of bag so that cord ends meet in the middle. Knot ends of cord tog to secure. 🍃

EUNNY JANG is the former editor of *Interweave Knits.*

Gossamer Stars Scarf

BY KAT COYLE

Delightful silk yarn and simple lace stitches play subtly with texture and light in the Gossamer Stars Scarf. Constructed from the center out with a provisional cast-on, bands of different motifs keep the knitting interesting but easy all the way.

Finished Size

11½" (29 cm) wide and 58½" (148.5 cm) long, after blocking.

Yarn

Fiesta La Luz (100% silk; 220 yd [201 m]/57 g): #3314 pecan, 3 skeins.

Note: If you cannot find a silk yarn, look for a bamboo, rayon, or viscose blend that will have the same slinky feel and relaxed drape.

Needles

Size 7 (4.5 mm). Adjust needle size if necessary to obtain the correct gauge.

Notions

Waste yarn; tapestry needle.

Gauge

21 sts and 25 rows = 4" (10 cm) in patt, after blocking.

Scarf

FIRST HALF

Using the invisible provisional method (see Glossary), CO 61 sts. Knit 1 row, purl 1 row. Work Rows 1–56 of Starlight chart 3 times, then work Rows 1–14 once more. BO all sts as foll: *Using the knitted method (see Glossary), CO 2 sts, BO 4 sts; rep from * until all sts are BO.

SECOND HALF

Remove waste yarn from provisional CO and place live sts on needle. With RS facing, join yarn and work Rows 1–56 of Starlight chart 3 times, then work Rows 1–14 once more. BO as for first half.

Finishing

Weave in loose ends. gently wet-block to finished measurements. 🖉

KAT COYLE lives in Los Angeles, California, with her family. She is the author of *Boho Baby Knits* (Potter Craft, 2007). Read more about her knitting at katcoyle.blogspot.com.

Starlight

(chart with rows numbered 1–55, odd rows labeled)

Legend:

- ☐ k on RS; p on WS
- • p on RS; k on WS
- O yo
- ╱ k2tog
- ╲ ssk
- ╲• p2tog
- ⋀ sl 2 as if to k2tog, k1, p2sso
- 🌢 p3tog, do not drop sts from left needle, yo, p3tog in same 3 sts, drop sts off left needle
- ☐ pattern repeat

Molly's Headband

BY PAM ALLEN

Molly's Headband's long rectangular shape is perfect for a panel of lace; a single repeat fits neatly down the center, and simple rows of eyelets along each edge add a pretty finishing touch. The headband begins and ends with a short length of I-cord for ties.

Finished Size

3½" (9 cm) wide and 15" (38 cm) long, not including I-cord ties.

Yarn

Frog Tree Alpaca Sport Weight (100% alpaca; 130 yd [119 m]/50 g): #96 light blue, 1 ball.

Needles

Size 6 (4 mm): Set of 2 double-pointed (dpn).

Notions

Tapestry needle.

Gauge

About 21 sts and 32 rows = 4" (10 cm) in St st. Exact gauge is not critical for this project.

Headband

With dpn, CO 3 sts.

I-CORD TIE

*K3, with RS facing slide sts to opposite end of needle, bring yarn around behind work into position to work another RS row; rep from * until I-cord measures 12" (30.5 cm) long.

LACE SECTION

Work Rows 1–16 of Headband chart once—19 sts after completing Row 15. Rep Rows 17–20 only until

piece measures about 13" (33 cm) from beg of chart patt, or 2" (5 cm) less than desired length for lace section, ending with Row 20 of chart. Work Rows 21–36 of chart once—3 sts; piece measures about 15" (38 cm) from beg of chart patt. Work I-cord tie on rem 3 sts until second tie measures 12" (30.5 cm) from end of chart patt. BO all sts. Weave in ends. Block headband to open up lace pattern. 🍃

PAM ALLEN is a former editor of *Interweave Knits.*

Headband

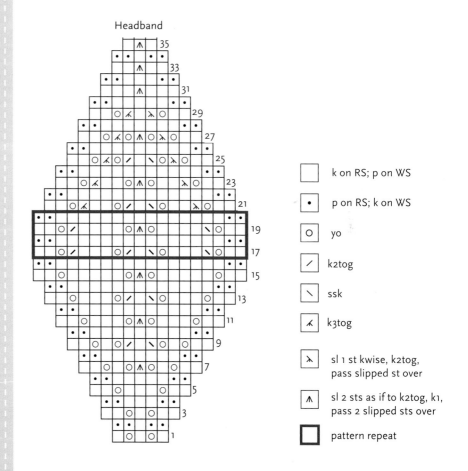

	k on RS; p on WS
•	p on RS; k on WS
O	yo
/	k2tog
\	ssk
⋏	k3tog
⋋	sl 1 st kwise, k2tog, pass slipped st over
⋀	sl 2 sts as if to k2tog, k1, pass 2 slipped sts over
	pattern repeat

Penobscot Silk Scarf

BY CYRENE SLEGONA

A single skein of silk yarn makes for an elegant little scarf, as the lace pattern fits neatly into a simple frame of stockinette stitch. For easy knitting, place stitch markers between the lace and stockinette sections.

Finished Size

5¾" (14.5 cm) wide and 41" (104 cm) long.

Yarn

Fiesta Yarns La Luz (100% silk;210 yd [192 m]/2 oz [57 g]): #3320 arctic ice, 1 skein.

Note: If you cannot find a silk yarn, look for a bamboo, rayon, or viscose blend that will have the same slinky feel and relaxed drape.

Needles

Size 6 (4 mm). Adjust needle size if necessary to obtain the correct gauge.

Notions

Tapestry needle; stitch markers (m).

Gauge

22 sts and 29 rows = 4" (10 cm) in St st.

Stitch Guide

Little Arrowhead Lace (multiple of 6 sts +1)

Row 1: (RS) K1, *yo, ssk, k1, k2tog, yo, k1; rep from * to end.

Rows 2 and 4: (WS) Purl.

Row 3: K2, *yo, sl 2 kwise as if to k2tog, k1, p2sso, yo, k3; rep from * to last 5 sts, yo, sl 2 kwise as if to k2tog, k1, p2sso, yo, k2.

Repeat Rows 1–4 for pattern.

Scarf

Loosely CO 33 sts. Working first and last st of every row in garter st (knit every row) for edge sts, work 7 rows even in St st, beg and ending with a RS row.

Next row: (WS) K1 (edge st), p3, place marker (pm), purl to last 4 sts, pm, p3, k1 (edge st)—8 St st rows completed.

Next row: (RS) K4, slip marker (sl m), work Row 1 of Little Arrowhead Lace patt (see Stitch Guide) over center 25 sts, sl m, k4.

Cont in established patts, working edge sts in garter st, center 25 sts in Little Arrowhead Lace, and rem sts outside lace patt in St st, until 7 reps of lace patt have been completed—28 rows total in lace patt. maintaining edge sts in garter st, work 8 rows even in St st, ending with a WS row. Rep the last 36 rows (28 lace rows followed by 8 St st rows) 7 more times—296 rows total from CO edge; eight 28-Row lace panels; nine 8-Row St st panels. BO all sts loosely.

Finishing

With yarn threaded on a tapestry needle, weave in loose ends. Pin scarf to measurements and mist lightly with water; allow to dry completely. 🍃

- -

CYRENE SLEGONA is a former member of the *Interweave Knits* staff.

A Stork's Nest Scarf

BY NANCY BUSH

In Estonia, storks and their huge nests (*kurepesa*) are a part of the springtime landscape. One often sees nests built on chimneys of farm buildings or on platforms constructed especially for these stately birds. This lace scarf is worked in the traditional Estonian Stork's Nest pattern, with an easy stockinette border keeping it simple.

Finished Size

About 9½" (24 cm) wide and 70" (178 cm) long after blocking

Yarn

Jojoland Cashmere, 100% cashmere yarn, laceweight, 400 yards (366 m)/2 oz (56 g) skein, 1 skein of #C244 Ice green

Note: If you cannot find a cashmere yarn, substitute another animal-fiber yarn with a slight halo, such as mohair or angora.

Needles

10" (25.5 cm) single point, size 4 (3.5 mm) or size needed to obtain gauge.

Gauge

19 stitches and 24 rows = 4" (10 cm) in lace pattern.

Notions

Markers; tapestry needle.

Scarf

Using the knitted method, CO 43 sts. Sl the first st of every Row purlwise wyf throughout. Knit 6 rows—3 garter ridges. Work Rows 1–12 of chart, placing markers for the garter edges as indicated. Rep these 12 rows 30 more times. Rep Rows 1–11 of chart once more. Work 6 rows in garter st. With WS facing, BO as follows: sl 1, *k1, k these 2 sts tog (as for ssk); rep from * until 1 st remains. Break yarn and pull it to fasten off.

Finishing

Pin to desired shape. Place a damp towel over the scarf to block. When dry, weave in loose ends. 🖋

NANCY BUSH, *PieceWork's* knitting contributor, teaches knitting workshops nationwide and owns the Wooly West, a mail-order source for knitters. She lives in Salt Lake City, Utah. She thanks Juta Kurman for permission to use the traditional Stork's Nest pattern, which originally appeared in *Haapsalu Rätik [Haapsalu Scarf]* (New York: Federated Estonian Women's Clubs, 1972).

Stork's Nest

	k on RS; p on WS
•	p on RS; k on WS
O	yo
/	k2tog
\	sl 1, k1, psso
∧	sl 2 as if to k2tog, k1, p2sso
ⱶ	sl 1 purlwise wyf on RS
V	sl 1 purlwise wyf on WS
	pattern rep
		marker position

Novel Sleeve

BY KATHY ZIMMERMAN

Protect your e-reader or small tablet in a novel way with this pretty
cover. Although it is worked up in sportweight cotton, you may find
a sportweight wool or wool blend easier to work. A single button
finishes it off.

Finished Size

About 5¾" (14.5 cm) wide and 8½" (21.5 cm) long, measured flat after blocking. To fit Amazon Kindle or similar-sized e-book reader.

Yarn

Halcyon Casco Bay Sport (100% cotton; 425 yd [388 m]/3.8 oz): #122 navy, 1 minicone.

Needles

Cover—size 4 (3.5 mm). I-cord closure loop—2 size 3 (3.25 mm) double-pointed (dpn). Adjust needle size if necessary to obtain the correct gauge.

Notions

Markers (m); tapestry needle; one ⅝" (1.5 cm) button or locking stitch marker for closure.

Gauge

27 sts and 37 rows = 4" (10 cm) in patt from Lace chart on larger needles, after blocking; 24 sts and 37 rows = 4" (10 cm) in seed st on larger needles, after blocking.

Stitch Guide

Seed Stitch (odd number of sts)
All Rows: K1, *p1, k1; rep from * to end.
Rep for patt.

Cover

With larger needles, CO 77 sts. Work lower border as foll:

Set-up row: (WS) Work in seed st (see Stitch Guide) to end.

Row 1: (RS) Work 19 seed sts, sl 1 pwise with yarn in back (wyb) for side, work established seed st over 37 front sts, sl 1 pwise wyb for other side, work 19 seed sts.

Row 2: (WS) Work 19 seed sts, p1, work 37 seed sts as established, p1, work 19 seed sts.

Rep Rows 1 and 2 three more times. Establish patt from Lace chart on front of cover as foll:

Next row: (RS) Work 19 seed sts, sl 1 pwise wyb, place marker (pm), work Row 1 of Lace chart over 37 sts, pm, sl 1 pwise wyb, work seed st over 19 sts. Cont in patt, slipping side sts on RS rows as established and working sts outside chart patt in seed st, until Rows 1–16 of chart have been worked a total of 4 times. Remove m on each side of lace patt and work top border as foll:

Row 1: (RS) Work 19 seed sts, sl 1 pwise wyb, work 37 seed sts, sl 1 pwise wyb, work 19 seed sts.

Row 2: (WS) Work 19 seed sts, p1, work 37 seed sts, p1, work 19 seed sts.

Rows 1 and 2 four more times. BO all sts in patt.

Finishing

Fold piece along slipped side sts, and sew selvedges tog at center back with yarn threaded on a tapestry needle. Sew bottom seam. Block to measurements.

CLOSURE LOOP

With dpn and RS facing, beg at center back seam, pick up and knit 3 sts along BO edge of cover. Work 3-st I-cord (see Glossary) for 2½" (6.5 cm). Sew 3 live I-cord sts to BO edge of cover on other side of seam—3 sts from each end of I-cord anchored on each side of seam. Weave in ends. Sew button in place on front side of top border or close with locking stitch marker. 🌿

- - - - - - - - - - - - - - - - - - - -

KATHY ZIMMERMAN is the owner of Kathy's Kreations in Ligonier, Pennsylvania. She enjoys working textured and lace patterns. She also enjoys reading her e-reader in her spare time, at the beach, or in her favorite chair.

Lace

Lace chart, 37 stitches wide, rows 1–15 (odd rows numbered 1, 3, 5, 7, 9, 11, 13, 15).

Legend:
- ☐ knit on RS; purl on WS
- • purl on RS; knit on WS
- O yo
- ╱ k2tog
- ╲ ssk
- ⋀ sl 2 as if to k2tog, k1, pass 2 slipped sts over

Rain on the Prairie

BY MAUREEN HEFTI

Lace first-timers take note: this beginner-friendly Rain on the Prairie Scarf dresses up simple eyelets with a luxurious yarn for a quietly elegant finished piece.

Finished Size

9½" (24 cm) wide and 42" (106.5 cm) long, after blocking.

Yarn

Buffalo Gold moon Lite (75% Tencel, 25% American bison down; 330 yd [304 m]/50 g): Tuscany, 1 skein.

Note: This yarn has been discontinued. Please substitute a laceweight (#0 – Laceweight) yarn that knits up to the same gauge.

Needles

Sizes 5 (3.75 mm) and 3 (3.25 mm). Adjust needle size if necessary to obtain the correct gauge.

Notions

Tapestry needle.

Gauge

25 sts and 40 rows = 4" (10 cm) in lace patt on smaller needles.

Note

* Slip first stitch of every row pwise with yarn in front. Before knitting the next stitch, bring yarn to back of work, making sure not to pull yarn too tightly (thus ensuring a flexible edge).

Scarf

With larger needles, loosely CO 58 sts. Change to smaller needles. Work in garter st (knit every row) until piece measures ½" (1.3 cm) from CO, ending with a RS row.

Rows 1, 3, 5, and 7: (WS) Sl 1 (see Notes), k3, p50, k4.

Row 2: (RS) Sl 1, k3, *k2tog, yo; rep from * to last 4 sts, k4.

Row 4: Sl 1, knit to end.

Row 6: Sl 1, k3, *yo, ssk; rep from * to last 4 sts, k4.

Row 8: Sl 1, knit to end.

Rep Rows 1–8 forty-seven more times—piece measures about 39" (99 cm) from CO. Work in garter st for ½" (1.3 cm). Use larger needle to BO loosely.

Finishing

Block to measurements. *Note: Tencel may be fragile when completely wet, so use care and do not stretch too tightly. Weave in ends.* 🍃

- - - - - - - - - - - - - - - - - - -

MAUREEN HEFTI lives in Sacramento, California, where she dreams of cold weather and warm woolen sweaters. She blogs about her adventures in knitting and life at ravenousknits.wordpress.com.

Lace Poncho

BY SUSAN STERNLIEB

Part poncho and part wrap, this garment is a good choice for an uninterrupted stretch of lace knitting. Dress it up with a slinky silk blouse or dress it down with a pair of jeans and turtleneck.

Finished Size

Rectangle measures about 16" (40.5 cm) wide (average) and 50" (127 cm) long, before sewing; edges of piece will be wavy.

Yarn

Joseph Galler Sahara (50% camel hair, 50% merino; 250 yd [228 m]/4 oz [114 g]): sharav (reddish brown), 2 balls.

Note: This yarn has been discontinued. Please substitute a worsted weight (#4 – medium) yarn that knits up to the same gauge.

Needles

Size 8 (5 mm). Adjust needle size if necessary to obtain the correct gauge.

Notions

Tapestry needle; pins.

Gauge

16 sts = 4" (10 cm) wide, and 32 rows (1 patt rep) = 5½" (14 cm) high worked in Ostrich Plumes chart, after blocking.

Poncho

CO 65 sts. Work Ostrich Plumes chart until Rows 1–32 have been repeated a total of 9 times; 288 rows completed; piece should measure about 50" (127 cm). BO all sts.

Finishing

Block to approximate measurements, allowing the fabric to curve into scallops on all 4 sides. Bring the BO edge around to meet lower 16" (40.5 cm) of long side edge, and pin in place with long side edge slightly overlapping BO edge. With yarn threaded on tapestry needle, sew pieces tog, sewing 1 or 2 sts in from selvedge of upper layer so that curved edge is left free, and not pulled straight by the seam. Weave in loose ends. 🖋

SUSAN STERNLIEB is a former member of the *Interweave Knits* staff.

	knit on RS; purl on WS		sl 2 as if to k2tog, k1, pass 2 sl sts over
╱	k2tog		
╲	ssk		pattern repeat
O	yo		

Ostrich Plumes

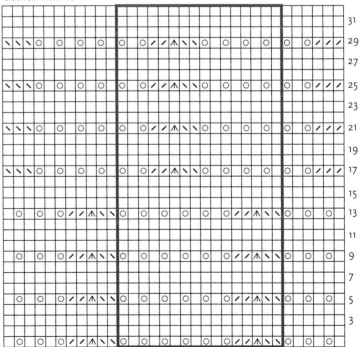

Peace Street Hat

BY GRACE AKHREM

Winter white yarn and red vintage buttons come together in a winter staple—the slouchy hat. Work the lace band flat, then picks up for the crown of the Peace Street Hat.

Finished Size

20" (51 cm) brim circumference and 11½" (29 cm) length.

Yarn

Shibui Knits merino Alpaca (50% baby alpaca, 50% Merino; 132 yd [121 m]/100 g): #7501 ivory, 2 hanks.

Needles

Brim: Size 6 (4 mm): straight. Body: Size 7 (4.5 mm): 16" (40.5 cm) circular (cir) and double-pointed (dpn). Adjust needle sizes if necessary to obtain the correct gauge.

Notions

One removable marker (m); five ½" (1.3 cm) vintage buttons; sewing needle and thread.

Gauge

19 sts and 27 rows = 4" (10 cm) in brim pattern on smaller needles; 17 sts and 25 rnds = 4" (10 cm) in St st on larger needle.

Note

* The brim of this hat is worked back and forth in rows. Stitches are picked up along the edge of the brim and the body of the hat is worked circularly.

Hat

BRIM

With smaller needles, CO 23 sts. Beg with a WS row, work Rows 1–19 of Brim chart once, then rep Rows 8–19 ten more times, work Rows 20–32 once, ending with a RS row. BO all sts kwise on WS, do not fasten off last st. Do not turn.

BODY

With WS still facing and larger cir needle, pick up and knit 69 sts along long edge of brim, ending 2½" (6.5 cm) before corner at opposite end (rem 2½" [6.5 cm] will form button flap)—70 sts. Turn.

Inc row: (RS) [K3, k1f&b, k2, k1f&b] 10 times—90 sts. Place marker (pm) and join in the rnd. Knit 21 rnds. Shape crown as foll, changing to dpn when necessary:

Rnd 1: [K8, k2tog] 9 times—81 sts rem.

Rnds 2–6: Knit.

Rnd 7: [K7, k2tog] 9 times—72 sts rem.

Rnds 8–11: Knit.

Rnd 12: [K6, k2tog] 9 times—63 sts rem.

Rnds 13 and 14: Knit.

Rnd 15: [K5, k2tog] 9 times—54 sts rem.

Rnds 16 and 17: Knit.

Rnd 18: [K4, k2tog] 9 times—45 sts rem.

Rnd 19: [K3, k2tog] 9 times—36 sts rem.

Rnd 20: [K2, k2tog] 9 times—27 sts rem.

Rnd 21: [K1, k2tog] 9 times—18 sts rem.

Rnd 22: [K2tog] 9 times—9 sts rem.

Break yarn, leaving an 8" (20.5 cm) tail and thread through rem sts. Pull tightly and fasten off.

Finishing

Weave in ends. Sew buttons onto garter border of button flap through both pieces of fabric. Block to finished measurements. 🍃

GRACE AKHREM has a strong passion for designing knitting patterns. When she isn't designing, she is either teaching or cooking. Learn more about grace on her website, graceakhrem.com.

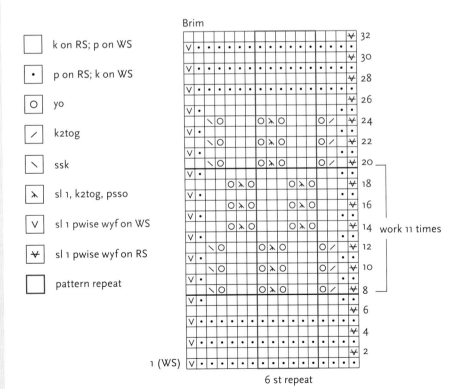

Chart legend:
- ☐ k on RS; p on WS
- • p on RS; k on WS
- O yo
- ╱ k2tog
- ╲ ssk
- ⋏ sl 1, k2tog, psso
- V sl 1 pwise wyf on WS
- ⱴ sl 1 pwise wyf on RS
- ☐ pattern repeat

Brim

work 11 times

1 (WS)

6 st repeat

A Scarf of Your Very Own

BY ANN BUDD

It's amazingly easy to design a basic lace scarf if you have a good stitch dictionary on hand and understand the mathematics of pattern repeats. Knitted in three vibrant colors of lightweight 100-percent Shetland wool, these scarves are meant to brighten up the gray days of winter and welcome in the blooming flowers of spring.

Finished Size

Fuchsia scarf: About 7½" (19 cm) wide and 64" (162.5 cm) long. Dark orange scarf: About 8" (20.5 cm) wide and 62" (157.5 cm) long. Bright yellow scarf: About 7½" (19 cm) wide and 64" (162.5 cm) long, blocked.

Yarn

Jamieson & Smith 2-ply jumper-weight Shetland (100% wool; 150 yd [137 m]/oz): #52 fuchsia, #125 dark orange, #91 bright yellow, 3 skeins each (one skein of yarn will knit about 20" [51 cm]).

Needles

Size 3 (3.25 mm).

Notions

Stitch holders; tapestry needle.

Gauge

24 sts and 36 rows = 4" (10 cm) in St st. Because these scarves don't have to "fit," exact gauge is not crucial, but will affect the finished dimensions.

Fuchsia Scarf

Loosely (hold 2 needles tog, if necessary) CO 51 sts. K1, p49, k1. Knitting the first and last st of every row, work according to Vine Lace chart on page 28 (foll red box for patt rep) until piece measures about 32" (81.5 cm) or half of desired total length, ending with Row 3 of chart. Break yarn and place live sts on holder. CO 51 sts as before and work another piece to match, ending with Row 1 of chart. Break yarn leaving a 36" (91.5 cm) tail. Using the Kitchener st (see Glossary), graft the live sts tog. Block, stretching out the points at the cast-on edges.

Dark Orange Scarf

Loosely (hold 2 needles tog, if necessary) CO 53 sts. K1, p51, k1. Knitting the first and last st of every row, work according to Fir Cone chart on page 28 (foll red box for patt rep) until piece measures about 31" (79 cm), or half of desired total length, ending with Row 15 of chart. Break yarn and place live sts on holder. CO 53 sts as before and work another piece to match, also ending with Row 15 of chart. Break yarn leaving a 36" (91.5 cm) tail. Using the Kitchener st (see Glossary), graft the live sts tog. Block, stretching out the points at the cast-on edges.

Bright Yellow Scarf

Loosely (hold 2 needles tog, if necessary) CO 51 sts. K2, *p11, k1; rep from * to last st, k1. Knitting the first and last st of every row, work according to Split Leaf chart on page 28 (foll red box for patt rep) until piece measures about 32" (81.5 cm), or half of desired total length, ending with Row 15 of chart. Break yarn and place live sts on holder. CO 51 sts as before and work another piece to match, also ending with Row 15 of chart. Break yarn leaving a 36" (91.5 cm) tail. Using the Kitchener st (see Glossary), graft the live sts tog. Block, stretching out the points at the cast-on edges. 🌿

ANN BUDD is the author of a number of knitting books, including The Knitter's Handy Book series and *Getting Started Knitting Socks* (Interweave, 2007). Visit her online at annbuddknits.com.

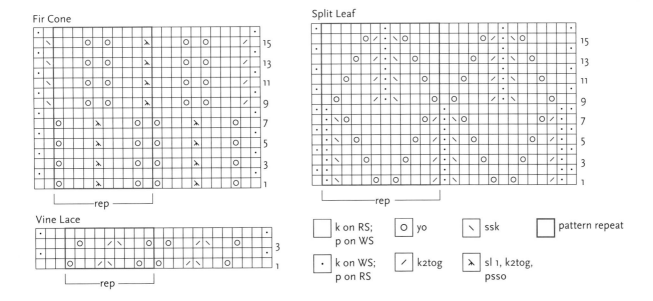

Fir Cone

Split Leaf

Vine Lace

	k on RS; p on WS
•	k on WS; p on RS
O	yo
/	k2tog
\	ssk
⅄	sl 1, k2tog, psso
	pattern repeat

Design a Scarf: A Beginner's Guide

Designing a scarf is very simple once you understand the principles of pattern repeats and gauge. If you haven't designed your own knitwear yet, a scarf is an excellent place to begin.

First decide the style of scarf you want to make and the type of yarn you want to use. Do you want your scarf long, thick, and luscious or light and airy? Is your primary goal warmth or fashion? Or both? Because the style is closely related to the yarn, you'll need to make these decisions simultaneously. Some knitters design a project around the yarn they want to use, others find yarn to suit a design concept. For the three scarves shown at left, I decided I wanted lightweight but not overly delicate lace, so I looked for sportweight yarn that could be blocked to emphasize the openwork.

If you don't have a specific stitch pattern in mind, take a few minutes to flip through a book of knitting patterns such as one of Barbara Walker's three treasuries. I found the stitch patterns for my scarves in *A Treasury of Knitting Patterns* (Schoolhouse Press, 1998). To simplify your knitting, look for stitch patterns that work all the stitch manipulations (increases, decreases, cable twists) on right-side rows, so that you can work every other Row carefree. Also consider the number of stitches in a pattern repeat. most scarves are relatively narrow and look best with small motifs repeated several times across the width. Because scarves are generally worn around the neck so that the right and wrong sides are visible,

reversible patterns or patterns whose "wrong" sides are attractive are ideal.

Most stitch dictionaries report stitch patterns as a specific number of stitches in a repeat with extra, balancing stitches. For example, the Fir Cone pattern used for the dark orange scarf repeats over 10 stitches and has 1 stitch for balance (so that the pattern looks the same at each selvedge). To work full pattern repeats, cast on a multiple of 10 stitches, then add 1 stitch for balance. (I wanted five repeats so I worked the pattern over 51 stitches.)

Once you've got an idea of the yarn and stitch pattern, knit a few generous swatches (at least 4 inches [10 cm] and two full pattern repeats square) to confirm that the yarn works with your stitch pattern and to determine the needle size and gauge that will give you the feel and drape you're seeking. Use the swatch for these needles to determine how many stitches to cast on based on your gauge, on the number of stitches in the pattern repeat (use full pattern repeats only), and on the width you want. This swatch will also help you decide whether you want to add a border to frame the stitch pattern and help prevent curling. Unless you choose a pattern that combines knit stitches and purl "bumps" in relatively equal proportions, such as garter stitch, seed stitch, or ribbing, the edges will curl. You can make such curling a design element or reduce the curl with a flat-lying edging. For my scarves, I wanted the lace pattern to dominate so I added just one edge stitch (garter) at each selvedge. One stitch generally isn't enough to prevent curling, but because I planned to block the scarves flat and because I didn't mind a little curling, I decided it would be adequate. many cable and lace patterns begun on the first Row and worked to the last Row of knitting will cause the cast-on and bind-off edges to ripple or scallop attractively. You can make such edges a design element, as I did with the lace scarves, or you can override such tendencies by working the first and last few rows in garter stitch, seed stitch, or ribbing. Knit another swatch to determine how wide you want

the edgings to be and add these stitches to the total number of cast-on stitches. (I cast on 53 stitches for the dark orange scarf: 50 stitches for five pattern repeats plus 1 stitch for balancing plus 1 edge stitch at each selvedge.)

Many stitch patterns are directional, appearing different from bottom to top than from top to bottom. To make the pattern look the same on each end of a scarf, work it in two sections joined at the back neck by seaming, binding off the stitches together, or grafting (joining live stitches together in a way that mimics a row of knitting; see Glossary). Seaming and binding off produce a ridge that you may or may not want. Though a bit more time-consuming, grafting produces a smooth, "seamless" join that makes a two-piece scarf look as though it's been worked in one continuous piece, while its two ends appear symmetrical.

ANN BUDD is the author of a number of knitting books, including The Knitter's Handy Book series and *Getting Started Knitting Socks* (Interweave, 2007). Visit her online at annbuddknits.com.

Zeva Oelbaum

Abbreviations

beg	begin(s); beginning	**pwise**	purlwise
bet	between	**RC**	right cross
BO	bind off	**rem**	remain(s); remaining
CC	contrasting color	**rep**	repeat; repeating
cm	centimeter(s)	**rev St st**	reverse stockinette stitch
cn	cable needle	**rib**	ribbing
CO	cast on	**rnd(s)**	round(s)
cont	continue(s); continuing	**rev sc**	reverse single crochet
dec(s)	decrease(s); decreasing	**sc**	single crochet
dpn	double-pointed needle(s)	**sk**	skip
foll	following; follows	**sl**	slip
g	gram(s)	**sl st**	slip stitch (sl 1 pwise unless otherwise indicated)
inc	increase(s); increasing	**ssk**	slip, slip, knit
k	knit	**ssp**	slip, slip, purl
k1f&b	knit into front and back of same st	**st(s)**	stitch(es)
k2tog	knit two stitches together	**St st**	stockinette stitch
kwise	knitwise	**tbl**	through back loop
LC	left cross	**tog**	together
m(s)	marker(s)	**WS**	wrong side
MC	main color	**wyb**	with yarn in back
mm	millimeter(s)	**wyf**	with yarn in front
M1	make one (increase)	**yo**	yarn over
M1R (L)	make one right (left)	*****	repeat starting point (i.e., repeat from *)
p	purl	******	epeat all instructions between asterisks
p1f&b	purl into front and back of same st	**( )**	alternate measurements and/or instructions
p2tog	purl two stitches together	**[ ]**	instructions that are to be worked as a group a specified number of times
patt(s)	pattern(s)		
pm	place marker		
psso	pass slipped stitch over		
p2sso	pass two slipped stitches over		

Glossary

Backward-Loop Cast-On

*Loop working yarn and place it on needle backward so that it doesn't unwind. Repeat from *.

Crochet Chain (ch)

Make a slipknot on hook. Yarn over hook and draw it through loop of slipknot. Repeat, drawing yarn through the last loop formed.

Crochet Chain Provisional Cast-On

With waste yarn and crochet hook, make a loose crochet chain (see above) about four stitches more than you need to cast on. With knitting needle, working yarn, and beginning two stitches from end of chain, pick up and knit one stitch through the back loop of each crochet chain (**FIGURE 1**) for desired number of stitches. When you're ready to work in the opposite direction, place the exposed loops on a knitting needle as you pull out the crochet chain (**FIGURE 2**).

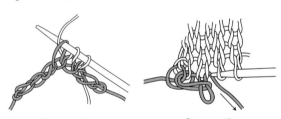

figure 1   **figure 2**

Invisible Provisional Cast-On

Place a loose slipknot on needle held in your right hand. Hold waste yarn next to slipknot and around left thumb; hold working yarn over left index finger. *Bring needle forward under waste yarn, over working yarn, grab a loop of working yarn (**FIGURE 1**), then bring needle to the front, over both yarns, and grab a second loop (**FIGURE 2**). Repeat from *. When you're ready to work in the opposite direction, pick out waste yarn to expose live stitches.

figure 1   **figure 2**

Kitchener Stitch (St st grafting)

Step 1: Bring threaded needle through front stitch as if to purl and leave stitch on needle.

Step 2: Bring threaded needle through back stitch as if to knit and leave stitch on needle.

Step 3: Bring threaded needle through first front stitch as if to knit and slip this stitch off needle. Bring threaded needle through next front stitch as if to purl and leave stitch on needle.

Step 4: Bring threaded needle through first back stitch as if to purl (as illustrated), slip this stitch off, bring needle through next back stitch as if to knit, leave this stitch on needle.

Repeat Steps 3 and 4 until no stitches remain on needles.

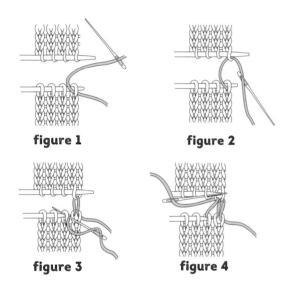

figure 1   figure 2

figure 3   figure 4

K2tog Bind-Off

With RS facing, k2tog, *return stitch on right needle to left needle without twisting it, k2tog; rep from *.

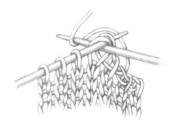

Knitted Cast-On

Place slipknot on left needle if there are no established stitches. *With right needle, knit into first stitch (or slipknot) on left needle **(FIGURE 1)** and place new stitch onto left needle **(FIGURE 2)**. Repeat from *, always knitting into last stitch made.

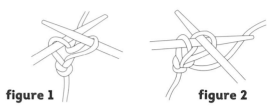

figure 1   figure 2

Mattress Stitch Seam

With RS of knitting facing, use threaded needle to pick up one bar between first two stitches on one piece **(FIGURE 1)**, then corresponding bar plus the bar above it on other piece **(FIGURE 2)**. *Pick up next two bars on first piece, then next two bars on other **(FIGURE 3)**. Repeat from * to end of seam, finishing by picking up last bar (or pair of bars) at the top of first piece.

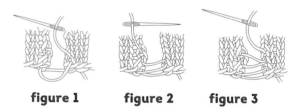

figure 1   figure 2   figure 3

Mattress Stitch for Garter Stitch

Step 1: Lay the two pieces next to each other, right sides facing up. Thread a tapestry needle with a length of yarn at least three times as long as the area you are sewing.

Step 2: Working from the bottom up, weave the seaming yarn from front to back on the bottom corner of one piece and then, from back to front, bring it through the bottom corner on the other piece **(FIGURE 1)**. Pull the yarn snugly to join the bottom edges.

Step 3: Insert the needle from bottom to top into the purl bump of a side stitch on one side. Bring the needle up through the bottom edge of the slightly higher stitch on the other piece. Continue sewing on alternate sides in this fashion until you finish the seam **(FIGURE 2)**. Pull tightly, and the two pieces should join seamlessly. Weave the yarn end into the seam for a few inches.

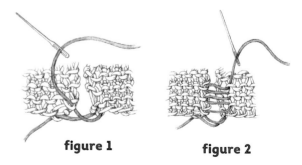

figure 1   figure 2

Purl 2 Together (p2tog)

Purl 2 stitches together as if they were a single stitch.

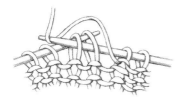

Raised (M1) Increases

LEFT SLANT (M1L) AND STANDARD M1

With left needle tip, lift strand between needles from front to back (FIGURE 1). Knit lifted loop through the back (FIGURE 2).

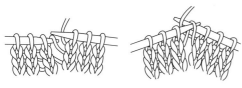

figure 1   figure 2

RIGHT SLANT (M1R)

With left needle tip, lift strand between needles from back to front (FIGURE 1). Knit lifted loop through the front (FIGURE 2).

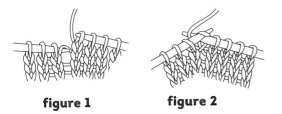

figure 1   figure 2

PURL (M1P)

For purl versions, work as above, purling lifted loop.

Short-Rows (Purl Side)

Work to the turning point, slip the next stitch purlwise to the right needle, bring the yarn to the back of the work (FIGURE 1), return the slipped stitch to the left needle, bring the yarn to the front between the needles (FIGURE 2), and turn the work so that the knit side is facing—one stitch has been wrapped and the yarn is correctly positioned to knit the next stitch. To hide the wrap on a subsequent purl row, work to the wrapped stitch, use the tip of the right needle to pick up the wrap from the back, place it on the left needle (FIGURE 3), then purl it together with the wrapped stitch.

figure 1   figure 2   figure 3

Single crochet (sc)

*Insert hook into the second chain from the hook (or the next stitch), yarn over hook and draw through a loop, yarn over hook (FIGURE 1), and draw it through both loops on hook (FIGURE 2). Repeat from * for desired number of stitches.

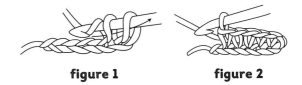

figure 1   figure 2

Slip, Slip, Knit (ssk)

Slip two stitches knitwise one at a time (FIGURE 1). Insert point of left needle into front of two slipped stitches and knit them together through back loops with right needle (FIGURE 2).

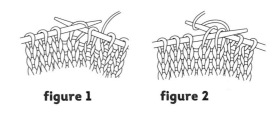

figure 1   figure 2

Standard Bind-Off

Knit the first stitch, *knit the next stitch (two stitches on right needle), insert left needle tip into first stitch on right needle (FIGURE 1) and lift this stitch up and over the second stitch (FIGURE 2) and off the needle (FIGURE 3). Repeat from * for the desired number of stitches.

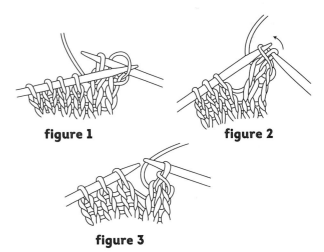

figure 1   figure 2

figure 3

Find popular patterns for quick and easy projects with these *Craft Tree* publications, brought to you by Interweave.

Crocheted Bags
ISBN 978-1-62033-579-6

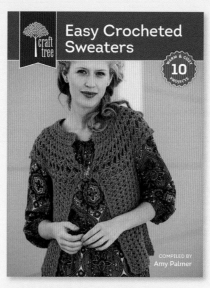

Easy Crocheted Sweaters
ISBN 978-1-62033-577-2

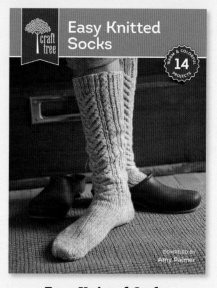

Easy Knitted Socks
ISBN 978-1-62033-574-1

Fast Crocheted Hats
ISBN 978-1-62033-578-9

Lace Knitting for Beginners
ISBN 978-1-62033-576-5

Quick Knitted Scarves
ISBN 978-1-62033-575-8

Visit your
favorite retailer
or order online at
interweavestore.com

INTERWEAVE®
interweavestore.com